Alpine Wildflowers

K. SUTTILL

J.E. (Ted) Underhill

hancock

house

ISBN 0-88839-975-8

Copyright © 1986 J.E. Underhill

Canadian Cataloging in Publication Data

Underhill, J.E., 1919—
Alpine wildflowers

(Wildflower series)
Bibliography: p
Includes Index
ISBN 0-88839-975-8

1. Wild flowers — British Columbia —
Identification. 2. Alpine flora — British Columbia —
Identification. I. Title. II. Series.
QK203.B7U53 1985 582.13'09711 C84-091580-2

Typeset by Jaine Bruce and Dorothy Forbes
Layout/production by Dorothy Forbes

Front cover photos: Subalpine meadow PARKS BRANCH PHOTO
Trollius laxus
Back cover photo: Dryas drummondii

Printed in Hong Kong

Published simultaneously in Canada and the United States by

HANCOCK HOUSE PUBLISHERS LTD.
19313 Zero Ave., Surrey, B.C. V3S 5J9
HANCOCK HOUSE PUBLISHERS INC.
1431 Harrison Avenue, Blaine, WA 98230

INTRODUCTION

If you have ever stood high on a mountain, above where the trees grow, then you will know there is a special feeling in being up there. You cannot find that same feeling anywhere else on land or sea. Perhaps it has something to do with the sweeping, panoramic views. Probably it is also because you sense that you are in a realm that is different, a part of the world where man scarcely lives. And, if you are there at the right season, you cannot help but be thrilled by the mountain's flowers.

Seen from the comfortable lowlands of the Pacific Northwest, the heights of our mountains appear to be difficult, bleak places. It is hard to visualize them as places where flowering plants thrive. Yet people who have once walked the trails beyond treeline go there again and again, and an important part of their pleasure is nature's alpine gardens.

From a plant's point of view mountain tops are different because of their severe climates relative to those at lower levels. The mountain top is colder yet gets more searing ultraviolet light from the summer sun, is exposed to the full fury of the winds, and generally has thin soils that dry in summer. Added to this, it is mantled with snow from about December until June or longer. Plants up there have a very short season in which to grow, blossom, and set seed, for the hard frosts begin in September.

It is not surprising that in this special kind of place there are many plant species that you will not find below. What is surprising is that amongst these are a few that do thrive 'way down along the coast. Whichever they are, the plants that grow here owe their success to the fact that they are adapted to the particular conditions high on the mountains. Many are hairy-leaved, a protection against water loss and burning summer sun; many have long root systems that can search deeply for water; many, especially on the dry rocks and ridges, are ground-hugging mats or cushions of growth, well able to dodge fierce mountain winds; still others have fleshy or waxy leather-like leaves to conserve moisture. All tend to bear a large amount of flower in relation to leaf surface. They don't need as much leaf up here.

Because of the short season between snowmelt and September frost these plants are compelled to bloom more or less at the same time. This is the major reason for the rich floral display so typical of the mountains. In the Pacific Northwest this flowering season is usually at its height in about the third week of July, but there are seasonal and local variations.

There are a few words in this book that require definition. First of these is the term "alpine," used alone, or as "alpine meadow." In order to provide an easy, workable definition for readers without training in biology, I have arbitrarily used the term "alpine" for everything above upper timberline, and have avoided reference to subalpine.

There are a few other words used applicable to the mountains: "talus" or "scree" is a slide slope of rock particles. A "fell field" is a stony alpine tundra area. The "snow-melt line" is the edge of the receding snow in spring.

Some plants, of course, occur both above and below timberline. In such cases their other zones of occurrence are noted where they are deemed significant.

With respect to plant description, heights given are for the alpine, as defined. If the same species grows at lower elevations it will likely grow taller there. The term "basal" means "of the base" and is used to describe leaves that arise at ground level, not up on the stem.

Virtually all the Latin names quoted are in accordance with Hitchcock, Cronquist, Ownbey and Thompson's "Vascular Plants of the Pacific Northwest," which is the principal reference for all the books in this series. Common names are mainly from the late Lewis Clark's "Wildflowers of British Columbia," but other works have been used as well.

Many people have the notion that one has to be young and husky to be able to enjoy the land above the trees. This is by no means entirely true. You can drive right to the alpine meadows at Manning Provincial Park in British Columbia, at Mount Rainier and Hurricane Ridge in Washington, and at Mount Hood in Oregon. These I have visited, but I know there are other roads, as at Mount Revelstoke and Blue Mountain—perhaps some roads that are a bit adventuresome. There is also chairlift access in the Rockies and elsewhere. It remains true that you can see only a very limited number of plant species around the parking lots. Fortunately, most of the places listed have easy trails, suitable for young and old, that lead to a variety of flowers.

This book is intended to help you identify most of the plants you are likely to find on such a walk. Carry it with you, because it will help you to look more closely, and to find more pleasure in your walk. Take your camera, too, for you will want pictures!

Stay on the trails, and please don't trample or pick or dig the alpine plants. Many of them are very fragile and slow-growing. Let's all be very careful to treat the alpine well, so that our grandchildren may enjoy it too.

ACKNOWLEDGMENTS

In a book of this type, and with size limitations, good pictures must be found to substitute for many words. My special appreciation is extended to Bill Merilees, Doug Leighton, Dennis and Kay Suttill, Keiron Gray, and Jessie Woollett, without whose pictures the book could not have been completed.

4

WESTERN ANEMONE
Anemone occidentalis

- herb, becoming 12 to 16 inches (30 to 40 cm.) at maturity
- often abundant on alpine meadows at snowmelt
- leaves finely divided and silvery-hairy

The mop-like seed heads earn this another common name, "Towhead Babies." It is very abundant on some Pacific Northwest mountains, usually blooming with Yellow Avalance Lily (p. 18) at the snowmelt line.

ALPINE ANEMONE
Anemone drummondii

- herb, to about 8 inches (20 cm.) at
  maturity
- dry ridges above treeline
- leaves divided and woolly-hairy

The flower, about an inch across, is
flushed blue on the backs of the sepals.
The seeds lack the tassels of Western
Anemone.

FRINGED GRASS-OF-PARNASSUS
Parnassia fimbriata

Also found in upland areas

- herb, usually about 8 inches (20 cm.)
- very moist places on alpine meadows
- leaves kidney-shaped, dark green, smooth

On mossy, wet places where snowmelt water trickles, this plant often forms large colonies. Nearby you may find the Globeflower and Marsh Marigold.

W. MERILEES

GLOBEFLOWER
Trollius laxus

Also found in upland areas

- herb, usually about 8 inches (20 cm.) at flowering
- wet alpine meadows
- leaves with 5 toothed lobes

The petal-like sepals are often tinged blue on the outside. They close to form a protecting "globe" in rainy weather—hence the plant's name.

7

W. MERILEES

MARSH MARIGOLD
Caltha biflora

- herb, usually about 6 inches (15 cm.)
- wet places on alpine meadows
- leaves rounded, shining, smooth, faintly toothed

As the name suggests, the flowers are usually in pairs. We also have C. *leptosepala* with longer leaves, and flowers borne singly.

SPRING BEAUTY
Claytonia lanceolata

Also found in sagebrush and upland areas

- herb, usually about 4 inches (10 cm.)
- open alpine slopes near the snow-melt line
- leaves 1 or 2, smooth, narrowly lance-like, fleshy

Flower color varies to pink, and there are varieties with yellowish flowers. The plant grows from a little edible corm, much sought by bears.

WHITE AVALANCHE LILY
Erythronium montanum

Also found in upland areas

- herb, usually 8 to 12 inches (20 to 30 cm.)
- timberline and on to the alpine meadows
- leaves 2, not marked, smooth

White Avalanche Lily spreads some spectacular carpets at timberline in the Olympics and in places in the Cascades. See also Yellow Avalanche Lily (p. 18).

W. MERILEES

MOUNTAIN AVENS
Dryas octopetala

Also found in upland areas

- mat-forming herb, usually about 4 inches (10 cm.)
- open stony ground, mostly above timberline
- leaves variably lance-like, deep-veined, edges rolled

Big feathery seed heads follow the flowers, and are almost equally attractive. See also the yellow *D. drummondii* (p. 30).

PUSSY-TOES
Antennaria lanata

- herb, from about 2 to 6 inches (5 to 15 cm.)
- dry open alpine slopes and ridges
- leaves narrowly spoon-shaped, and very woolly

Close inspection shows that this is actually a little daisy, with each chaffy "flower" consisting of a number of flowers. There are a number of kinds of *Antennarias* on our mountains.

MOUNTAIN SANDWORT
Arenaria capillaris

Also found in sagebrush areas

- tufted herb, usually about 6 to 8 inches (15 to 20 cm.)
- dry, open, rocky slopes and ridges
- leaves narrow and long

In our mountains are several species of *Arenaria*, some of which may be difficult to tell apart. The narrow leaves and star-shaped white flowers are common features.

COMMON SAXIFRAGE
Saxifraga bronchialis

Also found in upland areas

- tufted herb, usually about 8 inches (20 cm.)
- rock ledges and talus slopes, widespread
- leaves usually stiff, spiny-tipped and variable

A close look at the flower reveals a beautifully graded array of colored spots, from deep red to golden yellow.

KEIRON GRAY

KEIRON GRAY

SAXIFRAGE
Saxifraga adscendens

- herb, to about 4 inches (10 cm.)
- stony places and cliffs, Rockies, Cascades and Wallowas
- leaves often with three teeth, hairy

Our mountains, and those elsewhere in the world, hold a large variety of Saxifrages. The name translates loosely as "rock breaker." (See pp. 34 and 41)

ELMERA
Elmera racemosa

- herb, usually about 8 to 12 inches (20 to 30 cm.)
- talus slopes and rock crevices in the Olympics and Cascades
- basal leaves are kidney-shaped and stalked, blunt-toothed and hairy

Elmera is a relative of the Saxifrages mentioned previously and rather resembles the *Tellima* of the coastal lowlands.

PARTRIDGE FOOT
Luetkea pectinata

- mat-forming plant, usually about 4 inches (10 cm.)
- widespread above treeline on seasonally moist ground
- leaves mostly basal and deeply divided

Flower color varies to creamy yellow. The shape of a leaf is well described by the common name.

ALPINE SMELOWSKIA
Smelowskia calycina

- tufted herb, usually 4 to 6 inches (10 to 15 cm.)
- open, stony places in the alpine
- leaves mainly basal and blue-gray, mostly divided

Flower color may vary to purplish. The name commemorates a Russian botanist of the late 1700s and early 1800s.

ROCK JASMINE
Androsace chamaejasme
Androsace septentrionalis

- tufted herbs, to about 4 inches (10 cm.)
- seasonally moist screes and rocky soils
- leaves in basal rosettes, lance-like, hairy

Androsaces are small members of the Primula family. They are much more abundant on some mountains of Europe than they are here.

KEIRON GRAY

Androsace septentrionalis

Androsace chamaejasme

W. MERILEES

WHITE HEATHER
Cassiope mertensiana

- mat-forming plant to about 12 inches (30 cm.)
- rocky slopes and ridges
- leaves tiny and scale-like, and in 4 ranks

White Heather's bells of purest white contrast sharply with its dark evergreen foliage and red sepals. It seems to prefer the cool north-facing slopes for the most part. *C. tetragona* of our mountains is very similar.

D. LEIGHTON

OLYMPIC ONION
Allium crenulatum

- herb, usually about 4 inches (10 cm.)
- stony, seasonally moist open slopes
- leaves 2, strap-like, curved down and long

Shown is the color form I have met and photographed in the Olympics. The species does, however, vary to bright pink, and perhaps belongs in that section of the book.

YELLOW AVALANCHE LILY
Erythronium grandiflorum

Also found in upland areas

- herb, usually 6 to 12 inches (15 to 30 cm.)
- alpine meadows, flowering at snow-melt line
- leaves 2, unmarked, smooth and broad

Yellow Avalanche Lily will often push through the edge of the melting snow to greet the spring. The Western Anemone (p. 5) and Spring Beauty (p. 8) are its frequent companions.

MOUNTAIN BUTTERCUP
Ranunculus eschscholtzii

- herb, usually from 2 to 6 inches (5 to 15 cm.)
- moist alpine meadows and snow chutes above
- leaves mostly basal, 3-cleft, smooth and toothed

The photo shows the glistening flowers typical of the Buttercups. *Potentilla*, (see p. 22) which is fairly similar, lacks this waxy sheen.

COMMON MONKEY FLOWER
Mimulus guttatus

Also found in coastal and upland areas

- herb, variable, 4 to 24 inches (10 to 60 cm.)
- wet runnels on meadows or cliffs
- leaves variable, opposite, pointed, toothed

Colonies of this *Mimulus*, or of the red *M. lewisii* are fairly common by the snowmelt runnels on the alpine meadows just above timberline.

BROAD-LEAVED ARNICA
Arnica latifolia

Also found in upland areas

- herb, usually 8 to 16 inches (20 to 40 cm.)
- around trees at timberline, and beyond
- leaves variable, with long-stalked and lance-like basal ones

Arnicas in variety and abundance often huddle by the trees at timberline and by the rocks of the alpine meadows above. Their leaves are mostly in opposite pairs.

GOLDEN FLEABANE

Erigeron aureus

- tufted herb, usually about 4 inches (10 cm.)
- stony ridges and rock ledges
- leaves mainly basal, and spoon-like, with long stalks

Golden Fleabane, with its tidy habit, abundant flowers, and gray-green foliage is amongst the most appealing of our mountain flowers.

KEIRON GRAY

DWARF HAWKSBEARD
Crepis nana

- herb, about 2 to 4 inches (5 to 10 cm.)
- talus slopes and open stony ground
- leaves in a basal rosette, spoon-like, fleshy

Like other plants that grow on the shifting talus, this has a long, flexible root that permits it to delve deep for water, while the leaf rosette can shift with the rocks.

FRINGE-LEAF CINQUEFOIL
Potentilla flabellifolia

- herb, usually about 8 to 12 inches (20 to 30 cm.)
- alpine meadows to dry ridges, widespread
- leaves compound, with 3 toothed leaflets

As the name infers, the principal leaves bear some resemblance to little fans. The shrubby *P. fruticosa* grows on talus slopes and rocky areas in the mountains.

YELLOW COLUMBINE
Aquilegia flavescens

Also found in upland areas

- herb, usually 8 to 24 inches (20 to 60 cm.)
- alpine meadows and talus
- leaves are mainly basal and doubly compound

The foliage pattern is as beautiful as that of any plant. Leaves are of three leaflets, which, in turn, are of three lobed and toothed sections.

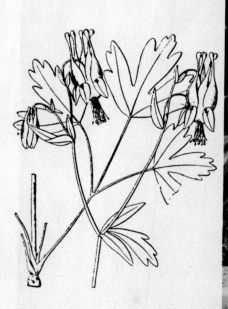

KEIRON GRAY

23

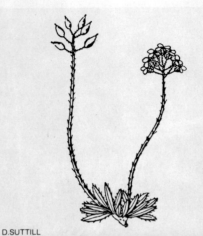

D.SUTTILL

DRABA
Draba spp.

- tufted or cushion plants, usually under 4 inches (10 cm.)
- rock crevices and stony ground
- leaves very small, usually hairy, often in rosettes

A variety of Drabas grow high on our mountains, most of them being difficult to identify as to species. Some make attractive ground-hugging cushions of growth, with the yellow or white flowers held just above.

MOUNT RAINIER LOUSEWORT

Pedicularis rainierensis

- herb, usually 12 to 18 inches (30 to 50 cm.)
- alpine meadows just above timberline
- leaves "fern-like," compound, leaflets alternate

In most alpine areas of the Pacific Northwest several kinds of *Pedicularis* may be found. All have similar "ferny" leaves and curiously formed flowers.

YELLOW MOUNTAIN HEATHER
Phyllodoce glandulifera

- herb, usually 8 to 12 inches (20 to 30 cm.)
- rock ledges and crevices and dry ridges
- leaves short (.5 to 1 cm.), linear, dark green

Flower color is often more yellow than shown here. This species sometimes hybridizes with *P. empetriformis* to produce hybrids of an intermediate color. (See p. 37)

PUSSY PAWS
Spraguea umbellata

- sprawling herb, usually about 2 to 3 inches (5 to 7 cm.)
- stony, open ridges near timberline
- leaves basal, fleshy, spoon-like, and dark green

Flower varies from a whitish color towards pink. *Spraguea* is related to *Claytonia* (p. 8) and to the *Lewisias*.

OVAL-LEAVED ERIOGONUM
Eriogonum ovalifolium

Also found in sagebrush areas

- tufted herb, usually about 8 inches (20 cm.)
- dry open ridges and talus slopes
- leaves variable and usually spoon-shaped, silvery-hairy

In alpine regions the flower color tends to age to reddish hues, a trait that is found in other *Eriogonum* **species.**

MOUNTAIN WALLFLOWER
Erysimum arenicola

- herb, usually about 8 inches (20 cm.)
- talus slopes and stony ridges
- leaves mainly basal, long lance-like, toothed

The particular variety illustrated grows only in the Olympic Mountains, but there are very similar *Erysimums* in other mountains of the Pacific Northwest.

Anemone occidentalis and Erysimum

STONECROP
Sedum lanceolatum

Also found in upland areas

- mat-forming herb, usually from 2 to 6 inches (5 to 15 cm.)
- talus and rocky slopes
- leaves very fleshy, often tinged red

Several species of stonecrop are common in the mountains. All tend to spread their mats of growth in suprisingly dry places.

YELLOW MOUNTAIN AVENS
Dryas drummondii

Also found in upland areas

- mat-forming herb to about 4 inches (10 cm.)
- dry ridges in the alpine
- leaves oval, dark, deeply veined, rolled edges

This species is also attractive as it matures its seed in big, tousled feathery heads. (See also p. 10)

ARTIC POPPY
Papaver radicatum

- herb, usually 4 to 6 inches (10 to 15 cm.)
- high rocky places
- leaves daintily cut, with segments overlapping

Poppies tend to be circumpolar in the arctic, only occurring southward in the high mountains. A few introduced species have escaped from cultivation in our lowlands.

KEIRON GRAY

MARTINDALE'S LOMATIUM
Lomatium martindalei

- herb, usually 4 inches (10 cm.) at flowering
- talus slopes and rocky places
- leaves beautifully cut, blue-green

Flowers are yellow, as shown, on the form that grows on the Olympic Mountains, but are whitish in the Cascades. As you may suspect from the foliage, *Lomatiums* are related to Parsley and Carrots.

MOUNTAIN GOLDENROD
Solidago multiradiata

- herb, usually 4 to 10 inches (10 to 25 cm.)
- high ridges and talus
- leaves mainly basal, spoon-like and smooth except on edges

Here is the dwarf mountain counterpart of the large Goldenrods that bloom in late summer in the valleys below.

SIBBALDIA
Sibbaldia procumbens

- herb, about 2 to 3 inches (5 to 7 cm.)
- dry, open ridges
- leaves compound, of three leaflets

Each leaf looks like a small, narrow version of a Strawberry leaf, and each leaflet is tipped with three teeth. The plant is not conspicuous, but is widespread and common.

W MERILEES

YELLOW MOUNTAIN SAXIFRAGE

Saxifraga aizoides

Also found in upland areas

- mat-forming herb, usually about 4 inches (10 cm.)
- damp, open ground in the mountains
- leaves small, linear, pointed and alternate

Although this is a widespread species, it scarcely occurs west of the Rocky Mountains in our area. Note the orange dots on the petals of most plants.

D. LEIGHTON

AGOSERIS
(False Dandelion)
Agoseris glauca

Also found in upland areas

- herb, usually 8 to 10 inches (20 to 25 cm.)
- alpine meadows and open ridges
- leaves long and narrow, with or without a few teeth

Yellow-fowered *Agoseris* **are found in the mountains of the Pacific northwest, but only a few range to above timerline.**

ORANGE HAWKWEED
Agoseris aurantiaca

Also found in upland areas

- herb, usually 10 to 12 inches (25 to 30 cm.)
- timberline meadows and ridges
- leaves slender, long, basal, sometimes toothed

The burnt orange color of the Hawkweed is unique, and makes the plant easy to identify.

INDIAN PAINTBRUSH
Castilleja spp.

Also found in coastal, upland and sagebrush areas

- herbs, variable, 8 to 16 inches (20 to 40 cm.)
- alpine meadows and open ridges near timberline
- leaves variable, often with three lobes

Indian Paintbrush occurs above timberline in a number of species, some of which are hard to tell apart, especially as they sometimes interbreed. In its scarlet, crimson and orange colors it is certainly a bold feature amongst the plants of the high country. Paintbrushes are partially parasitic, and obtain a part of their nourishment from the roots of other plant species with which they grow.

KEIRON GRAY

RED MOUNTAIN HEATHER
Phyllodoce empetriformis

- mat-forming shrubby plant, 4 to 12 inches (10 to 30 cm.)
- alpine meadows and rocky slopes
- leaves short, linear, very dark and stiff

Old mats of this Heather may grow to over twenty feet across. It seems to be at its best where it can find partial shade, as amongst scattered small trees just above timberline.

FEW-FLOWERED SHOOTING STAR
Dodecatheon pauciflorum

Also found in coastal and upland areas

- herb, usually 2 to 6 inches (5 to 15 cm.)
- mossy open runnels and talus
- leaves narrowly lance-like, held erect, smooth

At the base of the reflexed petals is a bright zig-zag line of deep orange. The snout usually also has some orange.

COLUMBIA LEWISIA
Lewisia columbiana

- tufted herb, usually about 4 to 8 inches (10 to 20 cm.)
- gravelly and stony open ground
- leaves basal, tufted, linear, pointed and fleshy

Flower color varies from nearly white to quite a deep pink shade. There are a number of local variants in different mountain areas, some having rounded leaf tips.

D. LEIGHTON

W. MERILEES

DOUGLASIA
Douglasia laevigata

- mat-forming herb, about 1 to 2 inches (2 to 5 cm.)
- high, stony ground and talus slopes
- leaves small (to 1 cm.), narrow, and strap-shaped

Douglasia laevigata **is probably most easily seen in the Olympic Mountains, where it is quite easy to find along the road towards Obstruction Point, and elsewhere.**

MOSS CAMPION
Silene acaulis

- mat-forming herb, to about 1 inch (2.5 cm.)
- high, rocky ground and talus slopes
- leaves very tiny and bright green

Tight cushions of Moss Campion seem to literally flow over the rocks. It is not a moss, of course, but a member of the Carnation family.

PURPLE SAXIFRAGE
Saxifraga oppositifolia

- mat-forming herb, to about 2 inches (5 cm.)
- high, rocky ground
- leaves in four ranks, narrow, stiff and about one inch long

Like most alpine plants, this one descends to lower levels at higher latitudes. Thus it is found along the shores of the Arctic Ocean.

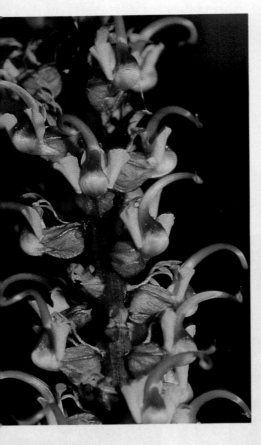

ELEPHANT'S HEAD
Pedicularis groenlandicum

Also found in upland areas

- herb, usually 12 to 18 inches (30 to 45 cm.)
- damp meadows near timberline
- leaves divided along a central rib, hence "fern-like"

This is one of the cases where the common name is truly appropriate, for it is easy to see the little elephant's head shape in each individual flower.

BIRD'S BILL LOUSEWORT
Pedicularis ornithorhyncha

- herb, usually about 8 to 16 inches (20 to 40 cm.)
- alpine meadows just above timberline
- leaves "fern-like," divided along a central rib

Foliage of this, and some other *Pedicularis*, is often flushed dark purple, especially when the plant first starts its season's growth. On many meadow areas several species are to be found.

ARCTIC LOUSEWORT
Pedicularis arctica

- herb, usually about 10 inches (15 cm.)
- high alpine herbmats
- leaves "fern-like", divided along a central rib

Pedicularis **are truly plants of the mountains, but this one is the high-climber amongst the group.**

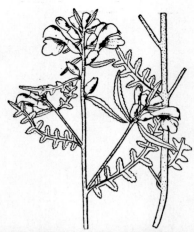

D. SUTTILL

STEER'S HEAD
Dicentra uniflora

Also found in upland areas

- herb, usually 2 to 4 inches (5 to 10 cm.)
- open, stony ridges near timberline
- 1 or 2 leaves, blue-green, and daintily divided

Steer's Head flowers briefly close on the heels of the receding snow. Its flower color makes it a bit hard to see amongst the rocks. Manning Park has some excellent patches.

MOUNTAIN DAISY

Erigeron perigrinus

Also found in upland areas

- herb, usually 10 to 20 inches (25 to 50 cm.)
- open meadows close to timberline
- leaves usually lance-like and fairly large

This is one of the commonest plants of many timberline meadows, but it does also grow in suitable places higher up. High level forms are smaller, with blunt leaves.

D. SUTTILL

BLADDER CAMPION
Lychnis apetala

- tufted herb, usually about 3 to 6 inches (7 to 15 cm.)
- dry stony slopes and talus
- leaves mainly basal, narrow, and pointed

The inflated calyx with its lines of purplish hairs is interesting and attractive, even when petals are not in evidence.

SPREADING PHLOX
Phlox diffusa

Also found in upland areas

- mat-forming herb, about 1 to 2 inches (2 to 5 cm.)
- open rocky ridges and talus slopes
- leaves are very small, narrow, recurved, and pointed

Where the *Phlox* grows abundantly, you can enjoy its rich honey-like aroma on a warm, still morning. Notice the long tube extending beneath the flower's disc.

ROSEROOT

Sedum roseum

- herb, usually 2 to 8 inches (5 to 20 cm.)
- seasonally moist, rocky places and talus slopes
- leaves fleshy, flattened, shape variable, sometimes toothed

Flower color varies from rose or red to purple, and the leaves are often color-edged as shown here.

KEIRON GRAY

D. LEIGHTON

BEARDTONGUE
Penstemon davidsonii

- creeping, woody plant, usually not over 4 inches (10 cm.)
- rock crevices and talus
- leaves small (about 1 cm.), leathery, variable in shape

This is a ground-hugging little plant of the high rocks found in the Coast and Cascade Mountains and the Olympics. There tend to be local races with some differences.

Lyall's Larch and a rocky crag at Cascades Summit

SILKY PHACELIA
Phacelia sericea

- herb, usually 4 to 8 inches (10 to 20 cm.)
- high screes and rocky ridges
- leaves silvery-hairy, divided along central rib

Silky Phacelia is distinctive with its "bottle-brush" columns of flowers. This effect is created by the way the pistils and stamens are held out on long colored filaments.

View along Wonderland Trail—Ranier

D. LEIGHTON

SAW-WORT

Saussurea densa

- herb, usually 4 to 8 inches (10 to 20 cm.)
- high, stony ground in the mountains
- leaves narrow, long, toothed, and woolly beneath

Though not easy, perhaps, to recognize as such, *Saussurea* is a daisy. It is said to have a pleasant scent, something quite unusual amongst daisies.

ALPINE ASTER
Aster alpigenus

- tufted herb, usually 4 to 8 inches (10 to 20 cm.)
- open fells and ridges
- leaves narrow, mainly basal, long and not toothed

Here is an Aster that certainly looks quite unlike its lowland relatives, apart from its flowers. It is common in the Olympic Mountains and the Cascades.

BLADDER LOCOWEED
Oxytropis podocarpa

- mat-forming herb, about 2 to 4 inches (5 to 10 cm.)
- stony alpine ridges in the Rockies
- leaves compound, hairy, 1 to 2 dozen narrow leaflets

The name is derived from the fat, reddish pods which contain the developing seeds after the flowers have gone. Examine the flower, and you will recognize that this plant is a member of the Pea family.

KEIRON GRAY

PIPER'S HAREBELL
Campanula piperi

- trailing herb
- rock crevices, only in the Olympic Mountains
- leaves small (1 cm.), smooth, sharply toothed

Piper's Harebell is one of the finest of a number of alpine plants peculiar to the Olympic Mountains. Such plants are termed "endemics."

HAREBELL
Campanula rotundifolia

Also found in coastal and upland areas

- herb, usually 6 to 12 inches (15 to 30 cm.)
- habitats various, often on seasonally moist ground
- lower leaves rounded, stem leaves linear

These nodding blue flowers, found, too, in the arctic, are also common in Europe and the British Isles.

ALPINE HAREBELL
Campanula lasiocarpa

- herb, to about 4 inches (10 cm.)
- high, rocky mountain slopes across British Columbia
- leaves more or less lance-like and sharply toothed

The flowers are very large for the size of this little plant, often being over an inch in length. Notice that they do not hang, as in common Harebell, but stand erect.

J. WOOLLETT

LOW MOUNTAIN LUPINE

Lupinus lepidus
Lupinus lobbii

- herb, usually 3 to 6 inches (7 to 15 cm.)
- dry open meadows and ridges
- leaves compound, about 6 leaflets, very silky-hairy

Note the interesting markings on the flowers, and the characteristic way in which the leaves are partly folded.

LITTLE-FLOWER PENSTEMON

Penstemon procerus
Penstemon tolmiei

Also found in upland areas

- mat-forming herb, usually about 3 to 6 inches (7 to 15 cm.)
- dry stony ground, Cascades and Olympics
- leaves usually lance-like, smooth, mostly basal

This is an alpine form of a *Penstemon* that is commonly found at the lower levels in the mountains throughout the Pacific Northwest.

ALPINE COLUMBINE
Aquilegia jonesii

- tufted herb, usually 2 to 4 inches (5 to 10 cm.)
- rock crevices and talus in the Rocky Mountains
- leaves small and tightly divided, and hairy

Rarities such as this should never be picked or dug. There is no real hope of keeping them alive in lowland gardens. Take only their pictures!

D. LEIGHTON

Alpine fell-field
at Mt. Rainier

ALPINE VERONICA
Veronica cusickii

- herb, usually about 6 inches (15 cm.)
- widespread on alpine meadows
- leaves in opposite pairs, oval, and smooth

Notice the conspicuously long styles that protrude to give the flower a fuzzy appearance. These are much shorter in *V. wormskjoldii*, an otherwise rather similar species.

WILD LARKSPUR
Delphinium spp.

Also found in coastal, sagebrush and upland areas

- herbs, mostly 6 to 12 inches (15 to 30 cm.)
- dry open slopes above timberline
- leaves few, mostly basal, much dissected

Wild Larkspurs in about twenty species grow from the coast to well above the timberline. Those in the lowlands may be several feet tall. Some species are difficult to identify.

ALPINE FORGET-ME-NOT

Myosotis sylvatica
Myosotis alpestris

Also found in upland areas

- tufted herb, usually 3 to 6 inches (7 to 15 cm.)
- open ridges and slopes at height
- leaves narrowly lance-like, round-tipped and hairy

At its best this little plant bears flowers of the most beautiful intense clear blue. It is quite variable, growing progressively taller at lower elevations.

W MERILEES

FALSE HELLEBORE
Veratrum viride

Also found in coastal and upland areas

- herb, usually 48 to 60 inches (120 to 150 cm.)
- damp meadows near timberline
- leaves large, soft-felted, strongly parallel-veined

Young leaves of False Hellebore invariably attract curiosity as they poke up in fat green spikes amongst the smaller plants. The plant is poisonous to eat.

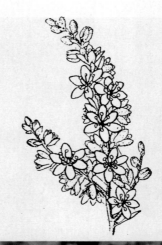

MOUNTAIN SORREL
Oxyria digyna

- herb, usually 6 to 12 inches (15 to 30 cm.)
- high rock ledges and talus
- leaves are basal, usually kidney-shaped, smooth, often reddish

Pale green flowers are followed by conspicuous clusters of disc-shaped reddish seeds. No other plant of our mountains is similar.

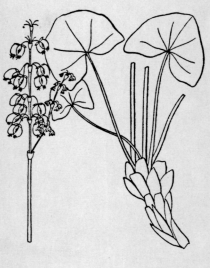

CROWBERRY

Empetrum nigrum

- evergreen plant, usually 4 to 6 inches (10 to 15 cm.)
- rocky or peaty places in the mountains
- leaves heather-like, small, linear, and very dark

The jet black berries have given the plant its name. In the north it grows at lower levels, and has been quite often sought as food.

BIBLIOGRAPHY

HITCHCOCK, CRONQUIST, OWNBEY & THOMPSON. *Vascular Plants of the Pacific Northwest* (University of Washington Press, 1964).

CLARK, Lewis J. *Wild Flowers of British Columbia* (Sidney, B.C.: Gray's Publishing, 1973).

PORSILD, A.E. *Rocky Mountain Wildflowers* (National Museums of Canada/Parks Canada, 1974).

HORN, Elizabeth L. *Wildflowers I — The Cascades* (Beaverton, Oregon: Touchstone Press, 1972).

TAYLOR, R.J. and DOUGLAS, G.W. *Mountain Wildflowers of the Pacific Northwest* (Portland, Oregon: Binford & Mort, 1975).

BUCKINGHAM, N.M. and TISCH, E.L. *Vascular Plants of the Olympic Peninsula* (University of Washington, 1979).

DAUBENMIRE, R. *Plant Communities* (New York: Harper & Row, 1968).

UNDERHILL, J.E. and CHUANG, C.C. *Wildflowers of Manning Park* (Victoria, B.C.: Provincial Museum and Parks Branch, 1976).

INDEX